21st Century
Skills Library

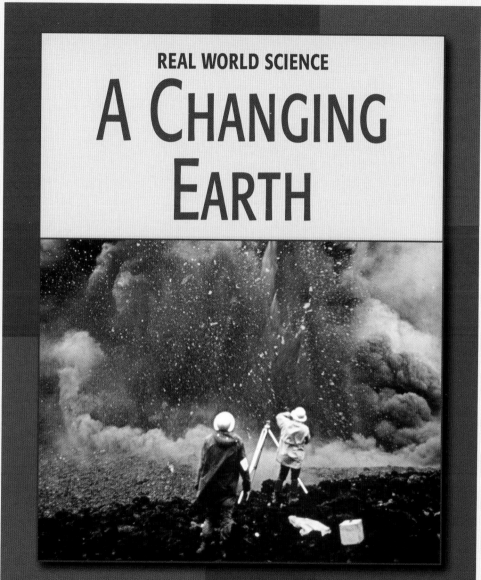

REAL WORLD SCIENCE

A CHANGING EARTH

Heather Miller

Cherry Lake Publishing
Ann Arbor, Michigan

Published in the United States of America by Cherry Lake Publishing
Ann Arbor, Michigan
www.cherrylakepublishing.com

Content Adviser: Laura Graceffa, middle school science teacher; BA degree in science, Vassar College; MA degrees in science and education, Brown University

Photo Credits: Cover and page 1, Explorer/Photo Researchers, Inc.; page 4, © Irina Kodentseva/Shutterstock; page 6, www.nps.gov/slbe; page 8, © javarman/Shutterstock; page 10, © M. Wassell/Shutterstock; page 12, Maury Aaseng; page 15, Creatas/Jupiter Images; page 16, Krafft/Photo Researchers, Inc.; page 18, Stephen & Donna O'Meara/ Photo Researchers, Inc.; page 20, Stephen & Donna O'Meara/Photo Researchers, Inc.; page 22, © Billy York/Shutterstock; page 23, Christian Darkin/Photo Researchers, Inc.; page 26, © Shutterstock; page 27, © iofoto/Shutterstock

Library of Congress Cataloging-in-Publication Data

Miller, Heather.
A changing Earth / Heather Miller.
  p. cm.—(Real world science)
Includes index.
ISBN-13: 978-1-60279-465-8
ISBN-10: 1-60279-465-0
1. Geodynamics—Juvenile literature. 2. Geology, Structural—Juvenile
literature. 3. Plate tectonics—Juvenile literature. I. Title. II. Series.

QE501.25.M55 2009
551.8—dc22   2008045697

*Cherry Lake Publishing would like to acknowledge the work of
The Partnership for 21st Century Skills.
Please visit www.21stcenturyskills.org for more information.*

TABLE OF CONTENTS

CHAPTER ONE

CHANGING LANDFORMS

The mighty Colorado River winds its way through the Grand Canyon. The river carved the canyon long ago.

Earth has been changing for billions of years. The powerful energy of

our planet has pushed mountains upward. It has opened canyons. **Erosion**

has smoothed rugged peaks. Volcanoes have raised islands out of the sea.

The earth may seem unchanging. But it moves and changes all the time.

Many powerful forces cause the earth to change. Running water is one example. It can slowly break down, or erode, solid rock. Rushing rivers, crashing ocean waves, and even rain all have this power.

The Grand Canyon in Arizona formed this way. The Colorado River slowly carved out the canyon. This took place over millions of years. The river slowly cut into the soil. Sand and pebbles were carried away by the river. As time passed, the river carried away more soil. Little by little, the canyon grew wider and deeper. Today the Grand Canyon is 15 miles (24km) wide, about a mile (1.6km) deep,

Windblown sand dunes are the centerpiece of Sleeping Bear National Lakeshore.

and over 277 miles (446km) long. The canyon is still being changed by

water and wind.

Wind is another force of nature that shapes the earth. Heavy gusts of

wind sweep up loose dirt and sand. Wind can change the shape of hills,

mountains, and other landforms. Sometimes sand collects into great

hills called **dunes**. Sand dunes form in places that have lots of sand and

wind. One such place is Sleeping Bear National Lakeshore in Michigan.

There, sand dunes rise more than 400 feet (122m) above the surface of

Lake Michigan. Gusts of wind come in from the lake. Sand grains are

pushed to the top of the dunes. With each gust, the dunes grow taller.

When the direction of the wind changes, the dunes change shape. The

changing winds move sand grains to new places. The tops of some

dunes are swept away and new dunes begin to grow.

REAL WORLD SCIENCE CHALLENGE

How does wind carry sand? Find out by using sand from the beach or in a sandbox. Find a patch of dry, loose sand. Place several rocks or shells just under the surface of the sand. Use a drinking straw to blow a direct stream of air over the sand. What happens? Now blow from a new direction. How does the movement of the sand change?

(Turn to page 29 for the answer)

Huge mountains of ice called **glaciers** also change the earth's surface.

Glaciers covered large parts of the earth thousands of years ago. Gravity

Runoff from melting snow and ice create a breathtaking view of Bridalveil Falls in Yosemite National Park.

pulled the glaciers down slopes and into valleys. Below the glaciers, giant,

sharp rocks rolled along. The rocks cut grooves into the earth's surface.

When the glaciers melted, they left behind valleys.

Glaciers changed Yosemite National Park in California long ago.

Yosemite Valley was once covered by glaciers. The glaciers covered the valley for more than 300,000 years. When they melted, they left behind

a U-shaped valley bordered by high, sharp cliffs. Waterfalls also formed

as melting snow rushed over cliff edges. This is how Bridalveil Falls

formed. Water drops more than 620 feet (189m) as it spills over the

rocky cliff.

REAL WORLD SCIENCE CHALLENGE

How powerful a force is ice? To find out, fill a plastic bottle with water and measure around the outside of the bottle. Place the bottle in the freezer overnight. Measure the outside again. What did you find?

(Turn to page 29 for the answer)

The world is covered with beautiful landforms. Some were created

by the wind. Others were formed by moving water or ice. All of them are

examples of the amazing powers of nature.

CHAPTER TWO

How Mountains Form

The jagged peaks of the Grand Tetons can be seen from miles around.

There are mountains on every **continent**. Three-fourths of the countries in the world are at least partly covered by mountains. Mountains form in different ways. The Himalaya Mountains in Asia are folded mountains.

Folded mountains form when heat and pressure change the earth's crust.

The crust is only a small part of the earth.

The earth is made up of many layers. The crust is the top layer. The thickness of the earth's crust is not the same in all places. Under the oceans, the crust is thinner. It is about 3 miles (5km) thick. On dry land, the crust is about 30 miles (48km) thick. But in some places it can be as thick as 62 miles (100km). The mantle is the next layer. It is made up of hot, liquid rock. The mantle is thicker than the crust. Scientists think the mantle is about 1,800 miles (2,900km) thick. The core is at the center of the earth. It is more than 2,100 miles (3,450km) thick.

21st Century Content

Some mountains are old and worn. The Appalachian mountain range in the United States is one of the oldest. The tallest mountain in the Appalachian range is Mount Mitchell. It stands 6,684 feet (2,037m) above sea level. The Himalaya Mountains in Asia are young mountains. They are still growing. Mount Everest is the tallest mountain in the world. It is in the Himalayan range. It is 29,035 feet (8,850m) tall.

The earth's crust is divided into several parts. These parts are called **plates**.

Plates are divided by huge cracks. There are seven major plates on earth. Each plate is thousands of miles wide. Plates float over the soft, not-quite-liquid mantle. They move very slowly. They move less than 1 inch (2cm) each year.

When two plates press against each other, pressure builds. Over millions of years, the pressure causes one or both of the plates to fold. These huge folds

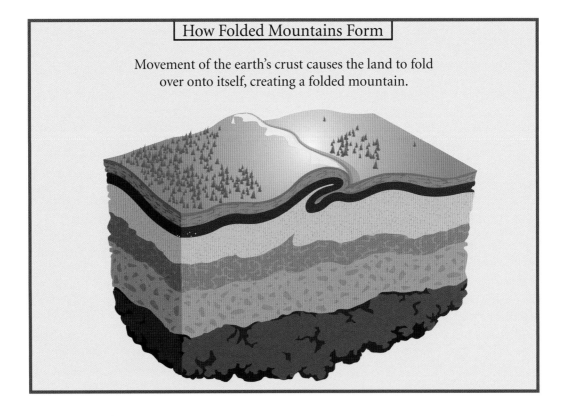

How Folded Mountains Form

Movement of the earth's crust causes the land to fold over onto itself, creating a folded mountain.

in the plates push upward. They sometimes appear as mountains. Mountains

that form this way are called folded mountains. The Andes Mountains in

South America are another example of folded mountains.

REAL WORLD SCIENCE CHALLENGE

Use a piece of paper to learn how folded mountains are formed. Place one
hand on each end of the piece of paper. Hold the paper flat. Slowly move
your hands together. What happens to the paper?

(Turn to page 29 for the answer)

Not all of earth's mountains formed this way. The Grand Tetons in

Wyoming are called fault-block mountains. These rugged mountains formed 10

to 13 million years ago. During that time the earth's crust cracked, rose, and fell.

This is how fault-block mountains form: The huge cracks in the earth's

plates are called **faults**. Faults divide the plates into smaller parts called blocks. Fault-block mountains are created when the blocks move. The

movement of the earth's crust can cause pressure to build. That pressure

can force the blocks to rise. When that happens, huge pieces of earth jut

upwards. Blocks of earth are stacked, and mountains are formed. Fault-

block mountains can also result from falling blocks. A block that sinks

below the earth's surface creates a low spot, or valley. The land around the

valley is now higher than the valley itself. It looks like a mountain.

REAL WORLD SCIENCE CHALLENGE

Use a map or search the Internet to identify and locate the mountain ranges in the United States. Are there more mountains on the eastern or western section of the United States? What is the highest mountain in the United States and where is it located?

(Turn to page 29 for the answer)

The Black Hills of South Dakota are small and rounded. These

mountains are called dome mountains. Dome mountains form when

The softly rounded mountains known as the Black Hills formed as magma seeped up through the earth's crust.

magma seeps up toward the earth's surface through cracks in the earth's crust. Magma is liquid rock that comes from the earth's mantle layer. As pressure builds, the crust sometimes heaves up. It then swells into a dome shape. As the magma cools it slowly hardens. A new mountain forms.

Mountains form in many ways. Because mountains rise from a variety of forces, they can look very different. The next time you visit a mountain, try to identify how it was formed.

CHAPTER THREE

Explosive Volcanoes

These volcanoes along the Aleutian Peninsula are part of the Ring of Fire, the circle of volcanoes around the Pacific Ocean.

In May 2003 the Anatahan volcano erupted. A huge plume of ash and steam shot more than 30,000 feet (10km) into the air. The blast ripped open a huge crater in the center of the volcano. Ash and steam sprayed into the air for many weeks.

Volcanoes can be found all over the world. Anatahan is in the Northern Mariana Islands. This group of islands is located in the Ring of Fire. The ring partly encircles the Pacific Ocean. Four hundred fifty-two volcanoes make up the ring of fire. That is more than three-fourths of all of the world's volcanoes.

REAL WORLD SCIENCE CHALLENGE

Use the Internet or a book at the library to find the Pacific Ring of Fire on a world map. Locate as many volcanoes as you can. How many states in the United States does the Ring of Fire affect?

(Turn to page 29 for the answer)

A volcano is an opening or crack in the earth's crust. Deep inside a volcano, magma is pushed up from the earth's mantle. Magma collects in an open space called a magma chamber. When the pressure inside the magma chamber becomes too strong, the nearby rock breaks open.

Magma is forced up through the opening. The opening is called a lava

tube. The lava tube runs up the center of the volcano. When the magma

reaches the surface it is called lava. Hot lava erupts and flows down the side

of the volcano. Lava can also spray high into the air. When the lava cools,

*Lava flows down the side of the Soufriere Hills volcano on
the island of Montserrat during a 1995 eruption.*

it falls back to earth. Large chunks of falling lava are called bombs. Smaller

pieces are called **cinders**. Even smaller dusty bits are called ash.

REAL WORLD SCIENCE CHALLENGE

This activity is messy but fun. Put about a teaspoon of baking soda into a clean, dry, 20-ounce (500ml) plastic bottle. Add a small squirt of dish soap. Pour about ¼ cup (60ml) of vinegar into the bottle. The vinegar causes the soda to bubble, sending a spout of bubbles shooting out of the top of the bottle. Try this experiment again using a bowl instead of a bottle. How did the reaction change? How is the bottle more like a volcano? How did the shape of the container affect the experiment?

(Turn to page 29 for the answer)

There are three types of volcanoes. One is a stratovolcano.

Anatahan is a stratovolcano. Stratovolcanoes are large and cone-shaped.

In stratovolcanoes, magma flows out through the lava tube. After one

erupts, the tube is plugged by hardened lava. The lava plug causes pressure

to build up again. When the pressure gets too high, the plug is blown out

Steam rises from a vent in the summit crater of Kilauea, one of the shield volcanoes that make up the Hawaiian Islands.

and the volcano erupts. Stratovolcanoes erupt with explosive force. Ash

and volcanic bombs can shoot 8,000 feet (2,438m) into the air.

The next type of volcano is called a shield volcano. The largest

volcano in the world is a shield volcano. That volcano is located in

Hawaii. It is called Mauna Loa. Shield volcanoes are very wide. Mauna

Loa takes up more than half of the island of Hawaii. Shield volcanoes are made from very fluid lava called **basalt lava**. In a shield volcano, basalt lava flows from a crack. It travels for a long distance before it cools and hardens. Over time a wide, low mound of lava builds up. Shield volcanoes tend to be very active. Large amounts of lava are spilled out each time one erupts. Shield volcanoes can be found in the ocean or on dry land. All of the Hawaiian Islands are shield volcanoes. Each one grew up from the ocean floor over millions of years.

The third type of volcano is a cinder cone volcano. These often grow out from the sides of larger volcanoes. They are the most common volcanoes on earth. The Mauna Kea volcano in Hawaii has about 100 cinder cone volcanoes on its slopes. Cinder cones are made up of piles of cinders. Lava shoots into the air during an eruption. The lava cools quickly

Cinder cones like these form when lava shooting into the sky cools, falls back to earth, and piles up.

and cinders form. The cinders fall back to the earth in piles. The piles of cinders form cinder cones. Cinder cones can be small or large. Some are only 33 feet (10m) high. Others grow to more than 300 feet (91m).

Volcanoes are extreme forces of nature. They can quickly change the earth's surface with one giant blast.

CHAPTER FOUR

DRIFTING CONTINENTS

*A computer illustration of Pangaea shows how the continents may
have been joined long ago as one huge supercontinent.*

The earth is made up of seven large pieces of land called continents.

Twenty-seven seas and four oceans divide the continents. But that

wasn't always the case. Scientists think that all of the land on earth was once connected. That was more than 200 million years ago. Scientists

call this connected landmass a supercontinent. They named it **Pangaea,**

which means "all earth."

REAL WORLD SCIENCE CHALLENGE

Can you make the continents fit together? Make a photocopy of a world map from a book or print one from the Internet. Cut out each continent. Study each continent's shape. Try to arrange the pieces to fit together as one large supercontinent. Do the pieces fit together perfectly? Does the outcome support Wegener's theory?

(Turn to page 29 for the answer)

A scientist named Alfred Wegener presented his supercontinent theory

in 1912. At the time, his idea seemed hard to believe. Scientists didn't think

continents could move. Today most experts agree that Pangaea really did

exist long, long ago.

There are many clues that help explain what happened to Pangaea. One clue can be seen on a flat map of the world. On such a map, the continents look a little like puzzle pieces that have been moved apart. South America looks like it slid away from the west coast of Africa. The top bulge of Africa seems to fit well with the east coast of North America.

There are more clues to this puzzle. Fossils of the ancient reptile *Mesosaurus* have been found in South America. Fossils of this same animal have been found in Africa. The animals could not have traveled across the ocean. This leads experts to think that the animals once lived on the same continent. Then the continents drifted apart. That is why the same fossils can be found on both sides of the ocean. Experts have also found matches like these with rocks and huge blocks of ice.

Today we know that the earth's crust is always moving. It moves across a sea of liquid rock. Scientists use special satellites to show the movement of the continents. A satellite that uses a laser has measured this movement. The Hawaiian island of Maui, for instance, moves toward Japan at the rate of about 3 inches (7.6cm) per year. Most continents move a little, but not more than about 6 inches (15cm) per year.

Experts have found the same types of dinosaur fossils on different continents. This suggests that the continents were once joined.

The Hawaiian island of Maui creeps just a little closer to Japan each year.

The movement of continents takes place underwater. Continents are

parts of much larger sections of crust called plates. The plates are divided

by huge cracks in the crust. The plates are always moving. On the seafloor,

magma flows up from the mantle through cracks. It is pushed outward.

The magma cools, creating new crust. The old crust is pushed back into

21st Century Content

More than 10,000 earthquakes occur each year in southern California. Most are so small that people don't even notice them. California's many earthquakes are easy to explain. The state sits on top of the San Andreas Fault. This is where the Pacific and North American plates meet. The San Andreas Fault is about 800 miles (1,287km) long. The total movement along the fault is less than 2 inches (5cm) per year but the tremors caused by the movement can be very strong.

the mantle, where it melts. The crust recycles itself like this over and over again. It is this process that keeps the plates in constant motion. The movement of plates is called **plate tectonics**. Scientists think that earth has been recycling itself since the beginning of time. They think this will continue far into the future.

REAL WORLD SCIENCE CHALLENGE ANSWERS

Chapter One
Page 7

When you blow through the straw, the grains of sand will move just like they do in the wind. Look closely to see how the individual grains move. The more you blow, the more sand is moved. As the sand moves, you will soon see the shells and the rocks reappear.

Page 9

As water freezes it expands. When you observe the bottle from the freezer you will notice that it has bulged out. That is because the ice inside takes up more space than the water before it was frozen. As water from melting glaciers trickles down into cracks and crevices on a mountain, it sometimes refreezes. When the water freezes, the ice expands and causes the rocks to move apart. Cracks grow wider and deeper. This movement caused by ice can also make rocks tumble down the side of a mountain.

Chapter Two
Page 13

When you move your hands together, the paper will rise up in the center. The rising peak of paper is similar to how mountains rise when the earth's plates are squeezed together.

Page 14

Some of the major mountain ranges in the United States include: the Brooks Range and the Alaska Range in Alaska; the Cascades in the Pacific Northwest; the Sierra Nevada stretch up and down California and Nevada; the Rocky Mountains, which run from New Mexico through Colorado and Montana and into Canada; the Appalachian Mountains are found in the east. There are also other mountain ranges in the western United States.

The tallest mountain in the United States is Mount McKinley in Alaska.

Chapter Three
Page 17

The Ring of Fire follows the basin of the Pacific Ocean. It begins at the southern tip of Australia, moves north past eastern Asia, curves across Alaska, then moves down the Pacific Northwest, and ends at the southern tip of South America.

There are 452 volcanoes located along the ring. The ring affects the entire West Coast of the United States. (Washington, Oregon, and California).

Page 19

When vinegar and baking soda are mixed, carbon dioxide gas is created in the form of tiny bubbles. The bubbles build up and flow out of the top of the container. The bottle is narrow, which causes the bubbles to squeeze together as they try to escape. This increases the pressure, which pushes the bubbles out of the bottle with more force. When the bowl is used, the bubbles are not squeezed together and the pressure stays low. The bubbles simply rise up and ooze over the sides of the bowl. The bottle is much like the lava tube of a volcano.

Chapter Four
Page 24

Answers will vary slightly as Wegener's theory is still debated. The eastern coast of South America fits well against the western coastline of Africa. The eastern side of the United States fits with the upper western lobe of Africa. The southwest portion of Asia fits against the northeast coast of Africa, while the northeast section of North America seems to line up with the western side of Europe and Asia. Antarctica, Australia, and India join together as one mass that seems to have broken off from the southeast coast of Africa. Remember, over millions of years, erosion, plate tectonics, earthquakes, and other forces of nature have changed the coastlines of all the continents. Because of these changes, the continents no longer fit together perfectly.

GLOSSARY

basalt lava (buh-SAWLT LAH-vuh) very fluid, hot melted rock that comes out of a volcano or crack in the earth's surface

cinders (SIN-durz) small pieces of cooled lava

dunes (DOONZ) large sloped hills of sand formed by the wind

erosion (i-RO-zhun) the gradual wearing away by water and/or wind

faults (FAWLTZ) large cracks in the earth's crust where two plates or sections of rock often rub against each other

glaciers (GLAY-shurz) large sheets or rivers of ice that move slowly down mountains or across valleys and plains

magma (MAG-muh) melted rock beneath the earth's surface

Pangaea (pan-JEE-uh) huge landmass thought to exist 200 million years ago that split into what are today's seven continents

plates (PLAYTS) sections of the earth's crust that make up the earth's surface

plate tectonics (PLAYT tek-TAWN-ix) theory that earth's surface is divided into large, thick plates that are always moving

FOR MORE INFORMATION

Books

Catherine Chambers and Nicholas Lapthorn, *Mountains*. Portsmouth, NH: Heinemann, 2007.

Neil Morris and Ann Morris, *Earth's Changing Continents*. Chicago: Raintree, 2004.

Ted Nield, *Supercontinent: Ten Billion Years in the Life of Our Planet*. Cambridge, MA: Harvard University Press, 2007.

Susanna Van Rose, *Volcanoes and Earthquakes*. New York: DK, 2004.

Web Sites

How Volcanoes Work
www.geology.sdsu.edu/how_volcanoes_work/Home.html
Tells all about types of volcanoes and what happens when they erupt

The Mountain Environment
www.woodlands-junior.kent.sch.uk/Homework/mountains.htm#define
Lots of great info on types of mountains, how they form, and much more

Paleomap Project
www.scotese.com/pangeanim.htm
Drag your mouse across the world map. See how the continents might once have fit together.

INDEX

ABOUT THE AUTHOR

Heather Miller is the author of more than 35 books for children. She lives in northeast Indiana, where she spends her time reading, writing, and teaching art to young artists. As a young girl she was fascinated by the wonders of science. She continues to be amazed by new scientific discoveries.